MW00834138

WORDS FOR THE HEART & SOUL

Poetry & Quotes

By:
Shereka Hill

Printed in the United States of America
Published: by Legacy Voice Productions

Cover Design by: Javeria Saleem

ISBN: 978-1-7351253-8-1

To contact author for ordering additional
copies, go to: rekahill2005@yahoo.com

Heartfelt Thank You's

I would like to thank my LORD and SAVIOR JESUS CHRIST. Without him nothing would be possible in my life.

I would like to thank my amazing husband and best friend William Hill, who is my biggest supporter. Thank you for always pushing me while supporting me. I love you.

To my awesome children Daesha, Nyeema, and Little William you all are and will always be my greatest motivation.

Lastly to all my readers who have chosen to pick up this book and read it, Thank you. I pray you find strength, encouragement, wisdom, and joy from my words. No matter what, never give up and always keep your eyes on God.

Own it, Believe in it, Walk in it

INSPIRATION

The hope we feel
The love we have
And the dreams we shared are an
abundance of inspiration.
You stretch out your hand and
extended it to someone else
That may be in need just to find that all
they needed was a helping hand.
Inspiration is obtained through
something that is more than yourself.
Finding it in the depth of your soul and
holding on to it like a pot of gold.
Life has its ups and downs going from
side to side, far or near, but in the end
what you see can be so much greater
than what you see so you have to follow
the inspiration to success and make it
through.
Even in the path of hardship and
downfall inspiration is what you have,
believing in it and persuading it until
the depth of the waters passes all

understanding while trusting in the word that has all understanding.

The greatest gift for a person is what they desire but inspiration is more than a gift, it is the sense of knowing that something out there is greater.

Searching for your hopes and dreams is a part of life but having the power of inspiration is powerful if you let it be because it's taking a chance on the faith that you can make a difference.

Inspiration is something that I strive to achieve everyday, wanting to let myself become free knowing that I have touched the lives of someone and set them free.

Not by my own will but through God's will and if I keep achieving that through inspiration then it will be my friend until the end.

Wrote 10-5-09

Courage is something that we all have but finding it in the midst of adversity helps to shape and impact your path

THE SEA

Looking out into the sea, what do you see, water's that stretch beyond the horizon. We are left to imagine what is out there, where it stops or begins. Inspiration is like the sea, it calms us while uplifting us because we can't see it, and we just feel it while owning it. Owning what you can't see and feeling it so deep that you have no choice but to believe in it. Believe in the possibility of the unknown, but walking out to the edge because you decided to take those steps of courage. Courage is feeling the strength to stay afloat like a current in the ocean, staying upbeat in the moment, in the pain, and in the sorrow all while reminding yourself constantly, that your future lies in your tomorrow. Many say, "tomorrow does not exist yet", which is true, but the inspiration in the depth of your soul says it does. Why? You have climbed so many valleys and faced so many lows on this journey that it was looking towards tomorrow that has sustained you and held you in the present. A present of not knowing what tomorrow will bring but being like that wave forever moving, growing, and pushing just to reach the depth of the surface. Being inspired and finding your inspiration is something we all seek but it is the power of Jesus Christ that makes the heart seek. Seek to find and do something bigger than yourself, allowing your gifts and talents to lead you to impact and motivate someone else. So be like the sea, continue to wait patiently as it runs through the earth ever so deep.

When you get to the mark you can appreciate the journey

UNBURDEN

As I reflect back on the past and the
choice that I made, I truly understand
the sacrifice I made then and how it
affects me now. I truly use this word
which tells a portion of my life that I
gave up my dreams, so that my
husband could take his flight. The
hidden treasures and wants of my heart
began to get lost as I became consumed
by my husband's and children's needs
and wants, and I began to fall apart. My
emotions and my thoughts started to
crumble as I sat back and wondered
who I was and where I was going. I felt
trapped and with no courage in sight,
eventually allowing the pain of
achieving something for myself
overtake me, as it swallowed all of my
might. My might to be strong and the
will to fight were gone, that at the end
of the day I truly decided no more.
Some-day's I wish for a quiet moment
or a day to myself. Where I can focus

on something that absolutely matters,
myself. As the days go on and I think
about the future I am always wondering
if I will ever get to that place that is
made just for me, where I have always
wanted to inspire the youth by helping
to set them free. Free from the burden
that tries to keep them from being
whole, but setting them on a path to be
inspired by God, the one who makes us
all whole. As I unburden my thoughts
on this page I still have the hope that I
will make it one day. Make it with the
help of God and his amazing grace,
with the loving man that God has given
me who stands with me in every way, to
the children that God has set before us,
I am constantly reminded that my path
will always have a plan and the burdens
of my heart will not always be forever
because it is just a season. A season to
wait, a season to be humble, and to be
patient because one day my flight will
take off, for reflecting on what has
strengthened me and will take me to

what will be because God has a plan,
for these burdens have helped shape
me. They will shape me into who I will
be while God is allowing me to fulfill
my husband's and children's wants and
needs by helping me to understand so
that I can be ready for the wants and
needs of the children and people I am
meant to impact. It's funny how I
thought it was a burden instead of
preparation for his mighty plan. I am
now living out my dream that I
desperately wanted and reflecting back
on how God foresaw this very moment.

Wrote 8-7-2012
Finished 5-20-21

I want you to take one step, then walk, and when you are ready to challenge your courage, Run

WHO'S IN BLUE

What happened to some who took the
oath who decided to put on the blue to
serve your community without any
hidden agenda. Who are you? Who do
you want to be? A person who serves
and uplifts or simply the one who tears
down and destroys. Destroying or
uplifting our society is a thought I pray
you think about when putting on the
blue because we don't want the
children of tomorrow to disregard you.
To disregard who you are and what you
are supposed to stand for, we know that
all lives matter because the world is
made up of so many different people
who just desire to live and be protected
while being surrounded with peace. If
we are going to fight, fight to win, fight
to restore the hearts of men, fight on
the right side for all lives. When you
put on the blue we don't just see you
we see someone who understands all

people in this world understanding that our cultures can be one and the same because at the end of the day we all have a heart that can be one in the same. We respect you, the ones who are in blue; it's the ones in blue that have decided to make up their own view. A view that is set apart from the true view which is the oath to serve and protect us all who are the ones that are in your clear view.

Strength is in your ability to survive

WHAT SOME GIRLS DO

Some girls do all kinds of things just to have a name, poke their chest out and walk the streets. There's no shame in their game.
They feel special when a boy tells them that they love them, but as they sit there about to have his baby they think to themselves is he really worth something.
Now they know that they have been having a game run on them, but it's too late because now the child is here and doesn't even know his father's name. Come to say what these girls do, they make a lot of mistakes, but they keep pushing on through.

Pray, Forgive, Restore

WHO IS OUT THERE

Pain, sorrow, hurt, distrust is all some people see because they are deciding to kill one of us creating a seize. One race that shares the same culture that some are too blind to even fully acknowledge our culture. A culture that is filled with so much depth and so much life that our souls shouldn't be so easily taken, like it's not worth a pot of gold. A life that shines so bright I do admit that it does not always reflect itself in the best light. But even in the dark or in the shadow that life still has a purpose and you have no right. No right to take, no right to abuse, no right to say whether or not that person shouldn't be excused. We are all puzzle pieces in this world that that can fit so right as we have a lot of growing up still left to do to get it right. A right we must take for our tomorrow because the future of our children is depending on us for their tomorrow.

Seek, Find, Live, Love

BLACK AS NIGHT

Why does he not show me any love
tonight
No kiss or a hug just the rejection of his
love
As I sit and wonder under the stars how
did I drift so far
Fear and the unknown scares me, all I
have is my soul to guide me
Love sometimes confuses me because
it has the power to consume me
On this darken night I look at the love
of my life, pulled into his might only to
be confused and loss; he has no clue of
my insight
He walks out into the dark looking for
me; he is on a purpose to prove that he
loves me
His feelings are just as strong but the
insecurities of my heart keeps me
abound from his love, will he be able to
prove to me that my heart to him is
where I will always belong

Only time will tell as he saturates my heart with his love, that it's only God and himself that I see alone

A heart that is broken is one that can be restored

A HEART THAT BLEEDS

My heart has been put to the test. I feel
the aftermath deep down in my chest.
Anger no longer holds me, but shields
me because the pain tries to consume
me. A heart that is so wide open that
you would think that it pours, but no;
the only thing that pours is the
disappointment and the hurt. There are
no more tears left to shed because I
have no voice. No voice to speak, to
shout or to even cry, all I have right
now is a heart that bleeds anguish as
I'm trying to cope with all the reasons as
to why. So as my heart bleeds, who do I
need and where do I find it? I know the
answer, it's in that BOOK, but will I
allow myself to read the book to stop
the bleeding or will I become an
unbeliever? Oh my, if that happens
then my heart will never stop bleeding
and the pain will never go away and
then HE will have the power to grab my
soul even more, always making me look

the other way. A way toward HIM that is filled with darkness so much that my soul will question the choice that I made forever. Changing my destiny in a good or a bad way. While my heart bleeds it's only time that can heal it, closing it slowly and carefully as my heart continues on while my soul rests steady in the comfort of HIS arms. Yes! I made my choice and it will always be HIM because HE made the heart, so therefore HE is the only one who can repair the heart to stop the bleeding. At the end of the day HE will always be what I needed.

CPSIA information can be obtained
at www.ICGtesting.com
Printed in the USA
LVHW021728270721
693795LV00001BA/23